SUSAN L. LINGO

Who's Who OBJECT TALKS

that teach about the OLD Testament

Ages 6-12

23 Cool Characters Your Kids will Love

Standard PUBLISHING

CINCINNATI, OHIO

DEDICATION

Listen, my dear brothers: Has not God chosen those who are poor in the eyes of the world to be rich in faith and to inherit the kingdom he promised those who love him?
James 2:5

Credits
Produced by Susan L. Lingo, Bright Ideas Books™
Illustrated by Paula Becker
Cover design by Diana Walters
Typeset/Design Assistant: Lindsay Lingo

All Scripture quotations, unless otherwise indicated, are taken from the HOLY BIBLE, NEW INTERNATIONAL VERSION®. NIV®. Copyright © 1973, 1978, 1984 by International Bible Society. Used by permission of Zondervan Publishing House. All rights reserved.

10 09 08 07 06 05 04   5 4 3 2
ISBN 0-7847-1311-1
Printed in the United States of America

CONTENTS

INTRODUCTION

When it comes to the Bible and its myriad of stories and characters, kids' two favorite questions are:

Who's who, and what did they do?

Do you know who was the oldest living person on earth or whose name is mentioned over one thousand times in the Bible? Or do you know whose name meant "star" and lived to became a superstar who saved her people? You'll discover these exciting answers plus loads more in *Who's Who Object Talks That Teach About the Old Testament!*

Who's Who Object Talks That Teach About the Old Testament combines life-changing Bible truths with loads of cool characters who make the Old Testament awesomely alive and relevant for kids today! Each message offers a memorable craft project, game, slick trick, or other concrete way to remember the who and the what behind each biblical person. And the nifty Who's Who collectible cards help kids recall in a snap who was who!

So have a ball presenting these memorable messages, fascinating facts, and awesome Bible enrichment fun to your kids as they memorably answer, "Who was who, and what did they do?" (Be sure to look for *Who's Who Object Talks That Teach About the New Testament* for even more fun and fascinating Bible characters!)

➤ **Who's Who Cards:** These small, collectible cards are found on pages 46-48. Simply make as many copies as there are kids in class and cut out the cards as needed. Let kids punch holes in the tops of the cards and attach them to notebook rings, key chains, or large paper clips for instant flip-through review. Consider using the cards in games and other activities.

➤ **Who's Who Name Board:** Decorate the edges of a sheet of poster board using colorful characters from an old Bible storybook or coloring book. Laminate the poster, then use dry-erase markers or erasable crayons to write each Bible character's name as he or she is being introduced at message time.

Who Was BALAAM ???
Numbers 22:21-23, 28, 31

Simple Supplies: You'll need a Bible, scissors, tape, magazines, several enlarged copies of the donkey head from page 45, and copies of the Who's Who Balaam card from page 46.

Before class, enlarge and cut out several donkey heads from the pattern on page 45. Color the heads gray or brown or run them off on colored construction paper. Cut out full-color mouths from magazine pictures. Choose mouths that are all about the same size and will fit on the donkey patterns you've prepared. (Cut out one mouth for each person.) Finally, write the name "Balaam" on the Who's Who board (directions on page 4) or on the chalkboard.

THE WHO & THE WHY

Tape donkey patterns to the wall, one pattern for every four or five kids. Have kids form four small groups and hand each person a magazine mouth and a piece of tape. Position the groups so each is standing opposite a donkey head and about five feet away. Explain that this game is played much like Pin the Tail on the Donkey, except you'll be pinning mouths on the donkeys. Have each child close her eyes (remind kids that peeking takes away the fun of the game), twirl in place a few times, then walk forward to tape the mouth on the donkey.

When everyone has had a turn to play, check out the humorous results, then give each other high fives. Say: **That was great fun with some funny results! The mouths on the donkeys almost look as though they could talk, but of course, donkeys never seem to have much to say.**

However, once in the Old Testament a donkey had a lot to say! You see, this donkey belonged to a man named Balaam. We've all heard that donkeys have a bit of a stubborn streak, but Balaam had a stubborn streak, too. Balaam was told by the king of Moab to go to the Israelites and curse them. Balaam asked God if this was his will, and God said, "No, do not curse the Israelites, for they are blessed." When Balaam told the king God's answer, the king would not accept that answer. So stubborn Balaam asked God again if he should curse the Israelites. This

time God said to go with the king but to say only what God told him to say. Balaam didn't want to curse the blessed people of God, but he climbed on his donkey anyway.

Down the road, an angel appeared, but stubborn Balaam was not paying attention, for he was thinking about what he would say to the Israelites. Balaam didn't see the angel, but Balaam's donkey did! She veered off the road, and Balaam beat her. "What a stubborn donkey," Balaam must have thought. Two more times the donkey stopped, and Balaam beat her. Finally, the donkey turned around and asked Balaam why he was beating her. Then Balaam saw the angel and repented because he had been blind. The angel gave Balaam a warning to say only what God told him to say. Balaam had learned that blind stubbornness can have terrible results if we don't accept what God tells us. And the donkey? She never talked again that we're told of—but she surely had spoken at the right time! Read aloud Numbers 22:31. Ask:

➤ *Who do you think made the donkey speak? Why?*
➤ *What might have happened to Balaam if the donkey had not spoken to him?*
➤ *How can we stay willing before God to do his will in the way he desires?*

Gently untape the mouths on the donkey and play the game once more. This time if someone tapes the mouth to the donkey, have everyone say, We can speak God's Word!"

Distribute the Who's Who Balaam cards and invite a volunteer to read the card aloud. Punch holes in the corners of the cards and add them to kids' Who's Who flip rings. If there's time, review any Who's Who cards previously collected.

Who Was DAVID?
2 Samuel 7:16

Simple Supplies: You'll need a Bible, paper plates, poster board, craft glue, plenty of plastic jewels (red, purple, green, and clear), scissors, satin cord, and copies of the Who's Who David card from page 46. *Before class, make a crown according to the illustration, then add jewels to the points of the crown. You'll also want to make* *a medallion from poster board. Decorate the medallion with jewels and attach satin cord so the medallion can be worn around the neck. If your kids are older or if you think paper plates won't fit their heads, make crowns from poster board instead. Older boys may wish to make medallions from poster board or thin foam board instead of crowns. Finally, write "King David" on the Who's Who board (directions on page 4) or on the chalkboard.*

THE WHO & THE WHY

Put on the crown and medallion you made earlier and gather kids in front of the Who's Who board or the chalkboard. Say: **Kings and queens of great renown always wear special crowns. They may also wear special medallions and medals. Why do you suppose kings and queens wore crowns and medallions?**

Pause for kids to share their ideas, then continue: **Crowns and medallions signified greatness and power. They were worn as decorations but, more importantly, to separate royalty from common people. Crowns, medals, and medallions were a sign of special greatness. But though King David probably wore a crown to rule his kingdom, he knew there was a much more important sign of greatness and power than crowns or medals. Before we discover what that is, let's make special crowns or medallions and explore who David was and why he was such a great king.**

Have kids quickly snip and form their crowns or medallion shapes (from paper plates or poster board). When the items are made but not yet decorated, say: **As we discover more about King David, we'll add colored jewels to the crowns and medallions. David appears in the Old Testament and was the youngest of the eight sons of a man named Jesse. Young David was a simple shepherd boy, but when God looked for someone to become king over his people, he looked at David and saw in him a heart that was pure, open, and honest. In fact, God called David a "man after his own heart"** (1 Samuel 13:14). **Glue a clear jewel to a point on your crown or medallion to signify David's pure heart.**

Pause, then continue. **As a young lad, David used his sling to kill the giant Goliath, who mocked God. David was also brave in his trust of God!** Add a red jewel to signify bravery and trust. **God chose David to become the greatest king of Israel and to rule his people with wisdom and love. King David united God's people into a great nation, and his reign lasted forty years. He was such a great and loved king that his rule is known as Israel's golden age. It was from the line of King David that Jesus was born many years later.**

Add a purple jewel to signify David's kingship and the royal line to Jesus, then continue: **And through his whole life, David thanked and praised**

God. He was like a living thank-you card to God! Add a green jewel to symbolize David's "living" thanks and praise of God.

Read aloud 2 Samuel 7:16, then ask:

➤ *What promise did God make to David?*

➤ *How did God's promise reveal what a great king David was? How did it reveal God's love for David?*

➤ *In what way did God's promise to David become a promise for Jesus' birth and our eternal life?*

Say: **David was such a brave warrior, wise king, and obedient servant of God that his name appears more than one thousand times in the Bible—more than any other name! And what was a more powerful sign of David's greatness than his crown? His love for the Lord, of course!**

Distribute the Who's Who David cards and invite a volunteer to read the card aloud. Punch holes in the corners of the cards and add them to the kids' Who's Who flip rings. If there's time, review any cards previously collected.

Who Was DANIEL?

Daniel 6:11, 13, 22

Simple Supplies: You'll need a Bible, a shoe box with a lid, scissors or a knife, a small flashlight, tape, and copies of the Who's Who Daniel card from page 46.

Before class, tape the lid to a shoe box. Cut a small peep hole in one end of the box and a small hole in the bottom at the opposite end of the box from the peep hole. Finally, write the name "Daniel" on the Who's Who board (directions on page 4) or on the chalkboard.

THE WHO & THE WHY

Hold the covered show box and place the flashlight beside you. Seat kids in a circle and say: **I have a box with a hole in the end. I'll pass the box and you can take a peek, but "shhhh"—don't let on what you see until everyone has had a turn to peek!** Pass the box and have kids each take a peep in the hole on the end of the box. (Of course, all they will see is darkness!) After everyone has had a turn to see in the box, ask kids what they saw.

Say: **You saw how darkness can surround the inside of this box and cover up anything we might see. But there is something that darkness**

cannot surround or cover up. What do you suppose it is? Let kids tell their ideas, then have them come up one by one to peek in the box as you hold the flashlight under the box and shine the light through the bottom hole.

Say: **Light chases away darkness, shining right through it! In Old Testament times, there was a man named Daniel who knew what darkness felt like but who also knew God's light cannot be surrounded or swallowed up by darkness. Daniel grew up in Jerusalem, where he was surrounded by loving friends and family and the freedom to worship and pray to God. But a king in a foreign country came and took many prisoners and sent them to live in a strange country called Babylon. Babylon was known for worshiping false gods—not the true God of Israel whom we love and worship.**

Daniel was probably a teenager when he was sent to live in Babylon, where he was surrounded again—but this time, he was surrounded by false gods and pagan people in a country he didn't know. Even in the midst of all this darkness, Daniel never gave up his faith in God. Daniel continued to pray even though he was sent to a lions' den for praying. God miraculously saved Daniel from the jaws of the lions. And when Daniel was an adult, he told kings what their dreams meant with God's help. Daniel spent his life surrounded by darkness in a pagan country, but he always continued to let the light of God shine through him to push that darkness away!

Read aloud Daniel 6:11, 13, 22. Then ask the following questions, tossing the flashlight to the volunteer answering the question. Have the light turned on as each question is answered.

> ➤ *Why do you think Daniel chose to serve God instead of the false gods of Babylon?*
> ➤ *How did Daniel's faith push away false gods, lies, and lions?*
> ➤ *In what ways did Daniel demonstrate his love for the one true God?*

Say: **Daniel lived his entire life in the bright light of faith, obedience, and love for God. And Daniel used God's light to shine on the people around him. Through Daniel, the kings and people in Babylon saw the power and might of the one true God— our God!**

If there's time, play a game of Shine the Light. Form a circle and choose someone to stand in the center and be "Daniel." Hand Daniel the flashlight. Choose another player to stand on the outside of the circle. Explain that the

Did You Know?

Daniel ate a healthy diet because he wanted to honor God by honoring his body. No burgers or fries for Daniel!

object is for the center player to pass the light to the player on the outside of the circle in two minutes or less—while kids in the circle attempt to block the pass. If the pass is made, choose two new players to pass the light. Continue until everyone has had a turn to pass the light.

Distribute the Who's Who Daniel cards and invite a volunteer to read the card aloud. Punch holes in the corners of the cards and add them to the kids' Who's Who flip rings. If there's time, review any cards previously collected.

Who Were The PROPHETS ???

1 Samuel 10:10; Hebrews 1:1, 2

Simple Supplies: You'll need a Bible, copy paper, a pencil, a paper lunch sack, and copies of the Who's Who Prophets card from page 48.

Before class, practice this simple demonstration to become familiar with how it works. Take a sheet of paper and imagine there are three rows of three squares. Using a pencil, number the imaginary squares in mixed order from one to nine, making number seven the center square. Carefully tear the paper into the smaller squares. (Notice that that only the center number 7 square has four torn edges!) Write the word "seven" on another sheet of paper.

Kids will draw the number squares from inside a lunch sack and keep them secret. You'll keep your number seven paper secret as well. Kids will be asked to hold their papers to their foreheads using one finger. Simply look for the four torn edges and call that child forward as you reveal the number on your paper, which will amazingly match the number on the square! Before class, write the word "prophets" on the Who's Who board (directions on page 4) or on the chalkboard.

THE WHO & THE WHY

Tell kids you have something amazing to demonstrate that will show that you have powers to predict outcomes. Hold a sheet of paper against the wall or chalkboard and write the numbers from one through nine in random order inside your invisible squares. (Be sure to make the center square number seven, but make it appear random.) Then tear the paper into the smaller squares and place them in the lunch sack. Tell kids you will write down a number from one to nine on a sheet of paper, then amazingly tell who has the matching number square. Write the word "seven" on your paper, then invite volunteers to choose squares from the sack as you turn your back. Have kids place the number squares face down on their foreheads.

Turn around and pretend to contemplate as you find the child holding the square with four rough edges. After a dramatic pause, call forward the child who is holding the correct square. Reveal your number sheet, then have the child reveal his square. (If kids want you to repeat the trick and you have time, choose another number for the center square.)

Say: **Wow! It almost seems that I know what is going to happen before it does or that I can see the future. But of course, only God knows the future, and sometimes he chooses people to become his messengers to reveal his will and plans to his people. In Old Testament times, God used prophets to warn his people when they were disobeying or when they were in danger. Sometimes God gave his prophets special powers so they could prove they were speaking for God and in his name. But more often, God's prophets**

2	4	8
6	7	3
1	9	5

were ordinary people who were given an extraordinary job—to take God's Word to his people. It sounds like an exciting job, doesn't it? But think about how it must have felt to tell people important news who didn't want to believe you or who became angry at you for telling such news. Would people really believe your message was right from God? Prophets didn't have an easy time, but they loved God and were chosen by God to serve as his messengers.

The Bible divides these special messengers into the major prophets such as Isaiah, Jeremiah, and Ezekiel and the minor prophets, who included Jonah, Micah, Malachi, and others. A good portion of the Old Testament is about the messages these prophets brought to God's people. One of the wildest of God's prophets was Ezekiel. The first message Ezekiel was to tell was on a scroll that he was instructed to eat. The scroll tasted "as sweet as honey" (Ezekiel 3:3). **What do you suppose this meant? It signified that the words Ezekiel spoke came from God and were good Unfortunately, the people didn't want to hear God's sweet words. So, to make his point, God had Ezekiel act out the messages they needed to hear. Let's see if you can act out some loving messages from God.** Choose volunteers to act out the following verses:

> ➤ *Deuteronomy 6:5: "Love the LORD your God with all your heart and with all your soul and with all your strength."*
> ➤ *Matthew 22:39: "Love your neighbor as yourself."*
> ➤ *Galatians 5:13: "Serve one another in love."*

Say: **Prophets were chosen by God to bring messages to his people.** Read aloud 1 Samuel 10:10 and Hebrews 1:1, 2, then ask:

> ➤ *Why were prophets disliked many times?*

> *In what ways did Jesus take on the role of a prophet in the New Testament?*

> *How can we carry the Good News about Jesus to others as he told us to do?*

Distribute the Who's Who prophets cards and invite a volunteer to read the card aloud. Punch holes in the corners of the cards and add them to the kids' Who's Who flip rings. If there's time, review any cards previously collected.

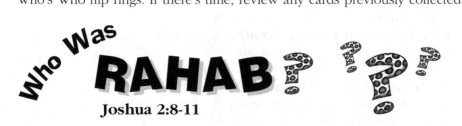

Who Was RAHAB?

Joshua 2:8-11

Simple Supplies: You'll need a Bible, thick red cord or ½-inch rope, scissors, rubber bands, newsprint, marker, tape, red construction paper, and copies of the Who's Who Rahab card from page 48.

Before class, cut cord or rope into three 24-inch lengths for each child plus one for yourself. On three sheets of newsprint, write the following words, one word per sheet: fear, faith, foolishness. On another sheet of newsprint, write the words belief, trust, courage (all on the same sheet of paper). Tape the words to the wall where kids can see them. Finally, write the name "Rahab" on the Who's Who board (directions on page 4) or on the chalkboard.

THE WHO & THE WHY

Join three cords together at one end using a rubber band. Invite a volunteer to hold the joined ends and begin to braid the three cords. As you braid, say: **Braiding is like weaving. You begin with three cords and end up with one. See?** Continue braiding the cord until you're about 4 inches from the end. Then attach a rubber band to hold the ends together.

Hold up the braided cord and say: **This cord reminds me of a powerful Bible person from the Old Testament. Her name was Rahab, and she helped God's soldiers in an amazing way. When Joshua's soldier spies came to Jericho to scope it out for their big attack before the walls came tumbling down, they needed a place to hide. The solider spies promised Rahab that if she helped them hide, God would save her life when the walls of Jericho came down. Rahab only knew God through what she had heard about his power and miracles. But she courageously helped the spies because she believed and trusted in God's power. Rahab hung a red cord out her window to tell God's soldiers where she was, and her life and her family's lives were saved!**

Rahab took three things and wove them into one. Who can read the three things Rahab wove into a solid cord? Invite someone to read the list of three words from the one sheet of newsprint on the wall. Then ask which of the three word cards shows what resulted from weaving belief, trust, and courage. Hold up the faith card and ask:

➤ *In what ways do belief, trust, and courage create and strengthen faith?*

➤ *How did Rahab prove her faith to God?*

➤ *What was Rahab's reward for having strong faith?*

Form pairs and distribute materials to braid or weave cords as you demonstrated earlier. As kids work together, say: **Rahab didn't have to see God to believe and trust in his power to save. Jesus told us in the New Testament that true faith means believing without having to see.**

Read aloud Joshua 2:8-11, then say: **Rahab believed and trusted God with her life—and she had the courage to act on her faith.**

When the braids are complete, cut index-sized cards from red construction paper and write the cards: "Belief, trust, and courage are woven into FAITH!" Tape the cards to the bottoms of the braids, then encourage kids to hang their braids on doors or walls as reminders of Rahab's remarkable faith in God and the example she gives us of the need to believe without having to see.

Distribute the Who's Who Rahab cards and invite a volunteer to read the card aloud. Punch holes in the corners of the cards and add them to the kids' Who's Who flip rings. If there's time, review any of the Who's Who cards previously collected.

Who Was METHUSELAH?

Genesis 5:25-27; Ecclesiastes 3:1, 2

Simple Supplies: You'll need a Bible, toothpicks, iced cupcakes or doughnuts, a birthday candle, squirty tubes of icing, napkins, and copies of the Who's Who Methuselah card from page 47.

Before class, make sure you have a cupcake or doughnut for each person plus two extras. Finally, write the name "Methuselah" on the Who's Who board (directions on page 4) or on the chalkboard.

Place a birthday candle in the center of a cupcake or on a doughnut. Hold up the cake and sing: **Happy birthday to you, happy birthday to you— happy birthday dear . . .** (stop singing, then continue). **Wait a minute! If we want to celebrate a special birthday, how many candles do you put on a cake?**

Pause for kids to respond, then say: **I only have one candle, and this birthday boy was pretty old. Let's use toothpicks as pretend candles. Then we'll discover who had the most candles on his cake in Old Testament times—or ever**.

Form two groups and hand each a cupcake and half a box of toothpicks. (Use the cake with the candle plus one extra.) Have kids place toothpick "candles" on the cakes for one minute and place as many as they can. Then stop and set aside the toothpicks.

Say: **Wow! You placed a lot of pretend candles on the cake, but I don't think we got close to the candles we need for a birthday celebration. You see, this birthday boy was named Methuselah, and he was the oldest living person. During Old Testament times Methuselah lived to be 969 years old! Imagine how old that is, when most people today live to be around 80 years old. In Old Testament times, when the world was fairly young, God allowed people to live many years. Adam lived to be 930 years old, Noah lived to be 950, and Abraham lived to be 175 years old. Why did God let people live so long back then? Well, remember that God is wiser than anyone, and he always has a plan for what he does. It was through God's plan and wisdom that Methuselah and others lived so long.** Read aloud Genesis 5:25-27, then ask:

➤ *Why couldn't we place enough candles on the cakes?*
➤ *How is this like having all people today live to be 960 years old?*
➤ *How does God's wisdom play a role in how long people live?*

Read aloud Ecclesiastes 3:1, 2, then say: **When the world was new, God allowed people to live long to build the world and accomplish his plans. But in his perfect wisdom, God knew that to have so many people live so long today would make the world too crowded—just as our cakes would have been too crowded with all of those candles. God gives us the time he sees fit, and in the time we live we can accomplish many great things for God. God's timing is always perfect, just as his wisdom is perfect. Let's celebrate Methuselah's birthday and our own lives in God's wisdom by decorating birthday cakes to enjoy.**

Let kids use squirty icing to decorate their cupcakes or doughnuts. Then distribute the Who's Who Methuselah cards and invite a volunteer to read the card aloud. Add the cards to the kids' Who's Who flip rings and review cards previously collected.

Who Was ABRAHAM???

Genesis 15:6; Hebrews 11:8-13

Simple Supplies: You'll need a Bible, a medium-sized box, newspapers, and copies of the Who's Who Abraham card from page 46.

Before class, collect a medium box. An actual moving box adds a fun element to this message. Make sure you have plenty of newspapers ready. Finally, write the name "Abraham" on the Who's Who board (directions on page 4) or on the chalkboard.

THE WHO & THE WHY

Set the moving box in the center of the room and place a stack of newspapers beside it. Form kids into two "moving teams" and name one group the "pacers" and the other the "unpackers." Have the packers stand beside the pile of newspapers and the unpackers on the opposite side of the box. Explain that when you say "go," the packers will crumple newspapers and toss them in the box. The unpackers must quickly remove the papers and smooth them out in a stack. Tell kids the object of the game is to keep the box empty. Explain that they'll have three minutes to play.

When the time is up, see if there are any papers in the box. Then have groups give each other high fives for a moving job well done. Say: **Moving is a lot of work and can be a bit scary, too. You don't know exactly what you'll find when you reach your new home, and there are so many things to pack and unpack. Just think if you were told to move but you didn't know where you were going! God told Abraham to pack up his family and move. Now most of us would worry about where we were moving. Or we wouldn't want to give up our comfy homes, or we wouldn't like the thought of so much packing and unpacking. But Abraham trusted God completely. So when God said move, Abraham moved!**

Abraham was born in the city of Ur in Mesopotamia. When God led Abraham out of Ur, he traveled with his family and flocks over one thousand miles on foot! That took a whole lot of footsteps for faith! And because of Abraham's great faith, God promised that Abraham's descendants

Did You Know?

Abraham's original name, the name he was born with, was Abram. God renamed him "Abraham," which means "ancestor of a multitude."

would grow into a great nation, which eventually became the twelve tribes of Israel.

Read aloud Genesis 15:6 and Hebrews 11:8-13, then ask:

➤ *In what ways did Abraham's great faith in God reveal his love for God?*

➤ *Do you think Abraham was afraid at times? Explain.*

➤ *Why do you think Abraham obeyed God and immediately moved upon God's command?*

➤ *What can we learn about faith and obeying God from Abraham?*

Play the moving game once more, this time switching roles. Then distribute the Who's Who Abraham cards and invite a volunteer to read the card aloud. Punch holes in the corners of the cards and add them to the kids' Who's Who flip rings. If there's time, review any cards previously collected.

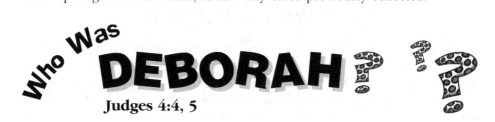

Who Was DEBORAH?

Judges 4:4, 5

Simple Supplies: You'll need a Bible, a gavel (or meat mallet), a black robe or jacket, a wooden or plastic box (large enough to stand on), and copies of the Who's Who Deborah card from page 46.

Before class, collect the items above and make sure the box is either sturdy enough to stand on or in. Kids will be using the box as a "soapbox." Finally, write the name "Deborah" on the Who's Who board (directions on page 4) or on the chalkboard.

THE WHO & THE WHY

Choose a volunteer to be the first "judge" and have her put on the black robe or jacket and hold the gavel. (The judge can be seated at a table or desk.) Choose another volunteer to be the "accused" and have him stand on or in the box in the center of the room and facing the judge. Have the rest of the class be the "jury" and seat them off to one side so they can see both the accused and the judge.

Explain that in this game, you will whisper a situation to the accused to act out and tell the judge. The judge will listen, then tell what should be done in this situation to show fairness. The jury will give either thumbs-up or thumbs-down signs to show their level of agreement with the judge's decision. For each majority that agrees with the judge, score one point and write a slash mark on the chalkboard or keep track on your fingers. Then choose new players to play the parts of the judge and accused (there may be two peo-ple accused). Use the following situations for the accused:

> *a pencil was taken because you didn't have one to use*
> *you forgot to repay the lunch money you borrowed from the teacher*
> *you and your friend* (need two players for the accused) *are in an argument because you broke her favorite game by accident*
> *you cheated on a spelling test because you didn't study the night before*
> *you and your friend* (need two accused) *are fighting over what game to play*
> *you and your friend* (need two accused) *are arguing over the last piece of pizza*

Did You Know?

Although Deborah was a wise judge and a brave soldier, she called herself "a mother in Israel" (Judges 5:7). What do you think she meant by this name?

When all of the situations have been role played, gather kids in a group and say: **Arguments, fights, and disagreements have been going on since the dawn of time. Because we're all human, we have a tendency to disagree, and sometimes we become blinded to the right answers because we're stubborn and don't want to admit we're wrong. That's why we need judges to help settle disputes.**

God appointed judges for the same reasons in the Old Testament before he decided to use kings. Judges were wise people who tried to find fair and logical solutions to problems. Deborah was one of God's bravest and wisest of judges. Deborah would sit under a special palm tree each day and wait. People would come to Deborah to present their problems and arguments and look to her for help. Deborah loved God and tried to help people when they sought her out, so it was natural that when God told Deborah to lead his people in battle, Deborah turned to God for his help.

Deborah's general was a man named Barak, but he was afraid to fight. So Deborah led God's soldiers in battle, and they won through God's power. Deborah then thanked and praised God for his help and power. Ask:
> *How did Deborah demonstrate great wisdom?*
> *In what ways did Deborah rely on God?*
> *How does relying on God when we face problems show our wisdom and bravery?*

Read aloud one final situation: **God has helped you solve the biggest problem in your life. What do you do now?** Let kids tell their ideas, then explain that you can offer a victory prayer as Deborah did. Join in a prayer thanking God for his wisdom, help, and power and asking for his help in coming to him when large or small problems face us.

Distribute the Who's Who Deborah cards and invite a volunteer to read the card aloud. Punch holes in the corners of the cards and add them to the kids' Who's Who flip rings. If there's time, review any cards previously collected.

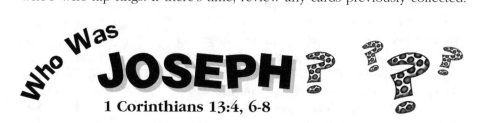

1 Corinthians 13:4, 6-8

Simple Supplies: You'll need a Bible, clear tape, a ¼-inch-by-18-inch dowel rod, a white crayon or chalk, markers, fishing line, and construction paper in the following colors: red, white, blue, purple, green, pink, orange, and black. You'll also need copies of the Who's Who Joseph card from page 47.

Before class, tape the construction-paper sheets lengthwise in two columns, four sheets per column and making the last colored piece the black sheet. (See the diagram on page 17.) Tape the end (opposite the end with the black sheet) of the paper to the dowel rod, then tie fishing line to the ends of the dowel rod to hang the colored banner. Finally, write the name "Joseph" on the Who's Who board (directions on page 4) or on the chalkboard.

THE WHO & THE WHY

Hang the colored banner on the wall or chalkboard and have the white crayon and markers handy. Tell kids the colored banner represents the colors of love but that there are words missing that teach us what love is and is not like. Read aloud 1 Corinthians 13:4, then have kids identify that love is being kind, patient, and humble. Write each of these words on a different colored square. Write the word "envy" on the top third of the black sheet using a white crayon, then put a slash through the word to show that love does not envy. Read aloud verse 6 and write the word "true" on a colored square and the word "evil" on the middle portion of the black paper and make a slash through the word "evil" to show that love does not do evil. Next, read aloud verse 7 and write the words "protects," "trusts," and "hopes" on three more colored sheets. Finally, read aloud the first sentence of verse 8 and write the word "fails" on the bottom portion of the black paper. Put a slash through the word to show that love never fails.

Read the colors-of-love list, then say: **These are important things that love does and does not do. Early in the Old Testament, we read about a man named Joseph who was the son of Jacob. Joseph had eleven** brothers, but he was the next to the youngest. As we discover more about Joseph and his brothers, let's see who had the colors of love and who didn't.

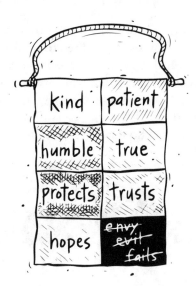

Jacob was Joseph's father, and he loved Joseph more than his other sons. Jacob gave Joseph fine gifts, including a coat with many colors. Most coats were just brown or plain because colored fabric showed wealth and riches. Ask:

➤ *Was it right for Jacob to favor one son over the others? Explain.*

➤ *Can we love and give to someone too much? Explain.*

➤ *How do you think the brothers felt about Joseph?*

Say: **Joseph's brothers were envious of Joseph!** (point to the word "envy" on the banner), **and they planned something bad for Joseph** (point to the word "evil" on the banner). **The brothers trapped Joseph in a well, then sold him into slavery in Egypt! Not very kind** (point to the word "kind"), **was it!** Ask:

➤ *According to our banner, how do we know the brothers did not love Joseph?*

➤ *How do you think Joseph felt about his family then?*

Say: **The brothers planned evil for Joseph, but God intended it for good! God blessed and protected Joseph in Egypt, and with trust and hope in God's love and his own patience** (point to the words "patient," "protects," "hopes," and "trusts") **Joseph became the official in charge of Pharaoh's grain. Many years later, a drought caused starvation in Joseph's homeland. Joseph's brothers went to Egypt to buy grain to eat. What do you suppose happened when the brothers and Joseph met? Joseph offered forgiveness to his brothers and helped them!** Ask:

➤ *Why did Joseph forgive his brothers and help them even after the brothers had been so wicked?*

➤ *How did Joseph demonstrate what love is all about?*

➤ *How did God's love sustain Joseph's own love?*

➤ *What do think Joseph's brothers learned about love from Joseph?*

Read aloud 1 Corinthians 13:4, 6-8. Say: **When we have genuine love in our hearts, love never fails us—even when evil surrounds us!** (Point to the word "fails" on the banner.) **Joseph knew true** (point to the word "true") **love because he humbly** (point to the word "humble") **accepted God's love in his heart and loved him back. Joseph's brothers and father learned** so much about love from Joseph, and in time their descendants grew into the twelve tribes that would make up the nation of Israel!

If there's time, let kids make their own colors-of-love banners to hang as reminders of what real love is and is not.

Distribute the Who's Who Joseph cards and invite a volunteer to read the card aloud. Punch holes in the corners of the cards and add them to the kids' Who's Who flip rings. If there's time, review any of the Who's Who cards previously collected.

Who Was JOB ?

Job 1:20-22

Simple Supplies: You'll need a Bible and three treats or small gifts for each child, such as note pads, pencils, wrapped candies, erasers, combs, coin purses, plastic rings or cars, crayons, or apples and cookies. You'll also need copies of the Who's Who Job card from page 47.

Before class, be sure you have three "neat treats" for each child. Finally, write the name "Job" on the Who's Who board (directions on page 4) or on the chalkboard.

THE WHO & THE WHY

Seat kids in a circle and silently hand each child three treats, making sure each person has the same as everyone else. Then look thoughtful and say: **Hmm ... let's make a few changes.** Begin switching treats and removing treats from some kids one at a time until some kids have many treats and some have only one or none. Allow kids to make comments such as, "Hey! Don't take that away!" or "I wanted that one!"

When the treats are mixed up, say: **Well, that's better! Is everyone happy now?** Encourage kids to express how they feel about how they've been "blessed" or taken from. Say: **You know, this reminds me of a man in the Old Testament named Job. As we discover who Job was, I will pause and say "give" or "take." If I say "give," hand one of your treats, if you have one, to someone beside you. If I say "take," take a treat from someone beside you.**

Job had so many blessings. He had a large family, huge flocks, much wealth, and his love for God. The whole world seemed happy and bright to Job. Give! Pause for kids to give a treat to someone, then continue: **Then one day, God decided to allow Satan to take everything away from Job,**

including his children, flocks, and wealth. **Take!** Pause for kids to respond. **Job's friends told him to curse God and turn from him. What do you think Job did?**

Pause for kids to tell their ideas, then continue: **Job didn't curse God. Job loved God very much and said, "The Lord gives ... give!** Pause for responses. **And the Lord takes away ... take!** Pause. **Praise be to God!" Even though Job had lost everything, he refused to hate God or turn away from him. Satan knew then that our love for God may be tested, but when we truly love God, nothing can turn us away from him! And Job learned that God is in control of everything and that God can do whatever he desires because he alone is God. In the end, God blessed Job with more children, flocks, and even greater wealth. Give!** Pause for kids to respond. Read aloud Job 1:20-22, then ask:

Did You Know?

God's prophet Ezekiel called Job one of the three holiest men who ever lived (along with Noah and Daniel)? Why was that a good description of Job?

➤ *How did Job show his love for God?*
➤ *In what ways did Job teach us about acceptance of what God plans for us?*
➤ *Why should we praise God in every situation even when it is hard?*

Redistribute the treats and let kids enjoy them. Say: **God is in complete control and is wise beyond what we can understand. Maybe God had a reason for allowing what seemed bad to happen to Job. And maybe God allowed bad to happen to teach us that what is really worth everything is our love and faithfulness to him—not wealth or worldly possessions. God is God and can do as he pleases. Our** *job*—notice that the spelling is the same as in Job's name—**is to praise God in all situations!**

Distribute the Who's Who Job cards and invite a volunteer to read the card aloud. Punch holes in the corners of the cards and add them to the kids' Who's Who flip rings. If there's time, review any cards previously collected.

Who Was NAOMI?
Ruth 1:15-17

Simple Supplies: You'll need a Bible, graham crackers, canned icing, squeeze-tube frosting, plastic knives, napkins, candy sprinkles, and copies of the Who's Who Naomi card from page 47.

Before class, make sure you have double graham crackers (the kind that can be broken in half). You'll need a double graham cracker for each child, since kids will be breaking them in half to share with a friend. Be sure you also have a plastic knife for each child. Finally, write the name "Naomi" on the Who's Who board (directions on page 4) or on the chalkboard.

THE WHO & THE WHY

Set out the napkins, graham crackers, plastic knives, tube frosting, canned icing, and candy sprinkles on a table. Invite kids each to decorate a graham cracker using the icing and sprinkles. As kids work, make comments such as "It's nice to have fun with our friends" and "Friends make everything brighter and cheerier."

When the crackers are finished, have kids find partners (a trio will work— kids can simply exchange cracker halves when it's time). Say: **Friends are so awesome, aren't they? We have fun with friends, tell them our deepest feelings, and even share our faith with them. In the Old Testament, we read about two of the best friends anyone could find. A young woman named Ruth married the son of a woman named Naomi. Naomi loved God and knew that Ruth didn't know who God was. So when Naomi's son died and Ruth was alone, Naomi and Ruth grew very close. Naomi taught Ruth about loving God and trusting in his care. Naomi taught Ruth that God is faithful to those who love him. In time, Ruth accepted God into her life and heart and loved him as much as Naomi loved him. And in return for Naomi sharing her love and faith, Ruth shared her food and home with Naomi!** Read aloud Ruth 1:15-17, then ask:

➤ *How does sharing our faith make our friendships stronger?*
➤ *How did Naomi show her love for Ruth? her love for God?*
➤ *What good things happened for Naomi after sharing her faith?*

Say: **Naomi was a wonderful friend who knew about sharing. And she knew that the best thing she could share with Ruth was her love for God! To remind you of how Naomi and Ruth shared, you can break your graham cracker in half and share it with your partner!** As kids share and enjoy their treats with their partners, discuss what other ways friends share with one another and why sharing God is the best way to show your friends you care.

Distribute the Who's Who Naomi cards and invite a volunteer to read the card aloud. Punch holes in the corners of the cards and add them to the kids' Who's Who flip rings. If there's time, review any cards previously collected.

Who Was GIDEON ? ? ? ?

Zechariah 4:6

Simple Supplies: You'll need a Bible, newspapers, a yardstick, and copies of the Who's Who Gideon card from page 46.

Before class, practice the following slick trick so you're familiar with how it's done. Place a yardstick on a table with a little over half of it hanging over the table's edge. Place a double sheet of newspaper over the yardstick on the table, as in the illustration. The object of this neat demonstration is to lift the newspaper off the table and yardstick without touching the paper. If you give the yardstick a hard "whap," the paper won't budge! But if you gently slap down on the end of the yardstick, the paper will flip upward quite easily. (Kids will naturally want to "muscle" the paper off the yardstick with a solid whap.) Finally, write the name "Gideon" on the Who's Who board (directions on page 4) or on the chalkboard.

THE WHO & THE WHY

Place the yardstick on the edge of the table and position the newspaper on top. Say: **Here's a puzzle for you. You need to catapult this newspaper off of the table and yardstick without touching the newspaper or blowing on it. You can only act on the yardstick to flip the paper. It looks like there are some strong types here, so who would like to try?**

Invite several volunteers to see if they can lift the paper. Allow each volunteer one attempt, then say: **It seems as if bigger muscles might do the trick, but we'll see in a moment. In the Old Testament, there was a simple farmer named Gideon who was called by God to be a strong warrior. Gideon and God's other people were being robbed of their food by their fierce Midianite neighbors. God told Gideon to battle the Midianites but gave Gideon only three hundred soldiers to face the thousands of enemy soldiers. Gideon asked God for signs to be sure he was doing the right thing. God answered, and Gideon trusted. But Gideon could not use force to do battle— he did not have enough soldiers.**

So instead, Gideon trusted God's power and led his soldiers to make a great noise and commotion in

the night that terrified the enemy. The Midianites ran away, and the farmers could finally live in God's peace! Gideon discovered that it wasn't by might that the battle was won, but by God's Spirit and ultimate power! Read aloud Zechariah 4:6, then ask:

> ➤ *In what ways did Gideon demonstrate his faith and trust in God?*
> ➤ *What did Gideon learn about God's wisdom and power?*
> ➤ *How can we place our trust in God more completely each day?*

Stand by the yardstick and newspaper. Say: **This slick trick is like Gideon's battle in that it isn't by strength or might that the newspaper can be moved, but by wisdom in how to move it.** Demonstrate how to gently slap the yardstick to flip the newspaper. Say: **This is a great reminder that what we do isn't always by sheer muscles or might, but by God's Spirit, wisdom, and power.** Let kids try to move the newspaper, then close with a prayer thanking God for his wisdom and asking for God's help in trusting his plans in defeating our own problems and "battles."

Did You Know?

The night before King Saul died in battle, Samuel's ghost appeared and predicted his death (1 Samuel 28). Once God's prophet, always God's prophet!

Distribute the Who's Who Gideon cards and invite a volunteer to read the card aloud. Punch holes in the corners of the cards and add them to kids' Who's Who flip rings. If there's time, review any Who's Who cards previously collected.

Who Was SAMUEL?

Proverbs 3:5, 6

Simple Supplies: You'll need a Bible, copies of the Scripture strip from page 44 (two for each child), scissors, rubber bands, copy paper, markers, tape, a wastebasket, and copies of the Who's Who Samuel card from page 48.
Before class, make and cut apart two Scripture strips for each child. Roll the strips and hold the mini scrolls closed with rubber bands. Write the following on sheets of copy paper, one phrase per sheet: "Tell it," "Keep it," and "Forget it." Tape the papers to three different corners of the room. Finally, write the name "Samuel" on the Who's Who board (directions on page 4) or on the chalkboard.

THE WHO & THE WHY

Place a wastebasket below the corner with the "Forget it" paper. Gather kids in the center of the room and hand each person a mini scroll. Tell them not to open the scrolls. Say: **You each have a secret message from a friend who wants you to tell the message. This is a very important message and decision, because telling the message will do two things: It will help people you do not know and will also hurt people you care about. What do you do with the message?** Point to the corners as you say: **Do you tell it, keep it to yourself, or toss it away and forget about it? Place your scroll in the place that tells what your decision would be.**

When the scrolls are placed, quickly count how many are in each corner, then hand kids the second mini scrolls. Explain that this time, the important message is sent from God, but everything else is the same: If you tell the message, it will hurt people you care about, but it will also help people you may not know. Have kids place their scrolls to indicate what they would do with the message. Count the results (most children will probably choose the "Tell it" corner, since the message is from God.) Then gather kids and ask:

➤ *Why did you make the decisions you made?*

➤ *If you chose to tell the message from God but not from your friend, why did you choose differently the second time?*

➤ *Were these tough decisions to make? Explain.*

Say: **We read in the Old Testament about a young boy named Samuel who had the same sort of tough decision to make. You see, Samuel's mother promised God that if he gave her a child, she would let the boy grow to serve God. So when Samuel was very young, he went to live with Eli, a priest who loved and trusted God very greatly.**

One night, God called Samuel while he slept and told him a very important message to tell. The message said that Eli's two sons were dishonest and should not be allowed to take Eli's place as Israel's leader. Imagine how little Samuel must have felt! He had a message from God to be told, but to tell it would hurt Eli even as it would help God's people. Samuel made his decision. He told Eli about his sons, and Eli decided to honor God's message. In time Samuel became the leader of God's people, and the Israelites recognized that Samuel was a prophet of the Lord. Samuel continued to listen to God and tell his people what they needed to hear. Late in his life, Samuel crowned Saul the first king of Israel, but when Saul became unfit to serve God, Samuel anointed David as the next king at God's request. When Samuel died, all of God's people were sad, for Samuel was the last of God's judges and the first prophet to advise the first Israelite kings. Ask:

➤ *How did Samuel show his love and loyalty to God even when it was tough?*

➤ *What might have happened if Samuel had not told God's message to Eli?*

➤ *How does obeying God go along with listening to what God says to our hearts?*

➤ *What does Samuel's life teach us about listening to God and obeying him?*

Have kids each open a scroll from the "Tell it" pile and read the important message. Then read aloud Proverbs 3:5, 6. Say: **We may not always understand what God is doing or why he wants us to behave in a certain way. But we do understand one thing for sure: We can lean on God and trust him always to lead us in straight paths!**

Distribute the Who's Who Samuel cards and invite a volunteer to read the card aloud. Punch holes in the corners of the cards and add them to the kids' Who's Who flip rings. If there's time, review any cards previously collected.

Who Was SAMSON ? ? ? ?
Exodus 15:2; Judges 16:28

Simple Supplies: You'll need a Bible, balloons, drinking straws, a permanent marker, masking tape, and the following "good-luck charms": a penny, a construction-paper four-leaf clover, and a rabbit's foot. You'll also need copies of the Who's Who Samson card from page 48.
Before class, collect the "lucky" items. Make three sets of pretend barbells from balloons and drinking straws. Blow up and tie off six balloons. Write "200 lbs." on each balloon, then tape the balloon knots to the ends of three drinking straws. Run a masking tape line across the center of the floor. Finally, write the name "Samson" on the Who's Who board (directions on page 4) or on the chalkboard.

THE WHO & THE WHY

Set the three barbells a few feet past the masking-tape line and have kids line up on the opposite side of the tape from the balloons and stand against the wall. Say: **Let's see how good you are at a special relay race! In this relay, you'll walk heel to toe to the masking-tape line, then hop across the line and pick up the heavy weights on the other side. You must carry the weights to the wall, then back to set the barbells in place and hop back over the masking-tape line. You'll then return to your team by walking heel to toe, and the next player in line will go. Oh, before we start, I have something that may help each team!** Hand the first person in each line one of the lucky objects. Say: **These lucky charms may help you do better! Be sure to pass your lucky item on to the next player in line when you're done with your turn!**

When everyone has had a turn to race, have kids sit in place. Collect the lucky items and say: **Wow! It sure helps to have lucky items, doesn't it— or is that what helped you in the race?** Ask:

➤ *Did the lucky items help you walk heel to toe? Explain.*

➤ *Can lucky items or charms help us be faster, better, or stronger? Why not?*

Say: **It's silly to put our faith in lucky pennies, a rabbit's foot, or any other "good-luck charm." They're silly and don't do a thing for us! In the Old Testament, a judge named Samson discovered that the real source of strength is God, not some lucky item. You see, Samson was a man dedicated to God, and he had promised God that he would serve God and keep himself holy and clean. Samson was a Nazirite, and as a sign of his special promise to God, Samson never cut his hair or drank alcohol. Samson was a very strong warrior for God and spent his life fighting the enemies of God's people—the Philistines. The Philistines wanted to know where Samson's strength came from, so they bribed a beautiful woman named Delilah to find out. Delilah was beautiful, and Samson fell in love with her—or so he thought! One night, Samson was tricked by Delilah, and he told her that his strength was in his hair. So Delilah had a man cut Samson's hair while he was asleep! Immediately Samson's strength was gone, and he was captured. Samson was blinded by the Philistines and turned into a slave held in chains.**

➤ *How do you think God felt when Samson broke his promise never to cut his hair?*

➤ *Where do you think Samson's strength was?*

Say: **Samson was convinced his strength was in his hair, but as the days and months went by and Samson's hair grew back—his strength did not. Samson was so sorry for what he had done. He loved God and knew his broken promises hurt God terribly. Samson told God he was sorry and asked for one more chance to serve him. The Philistines planned a huge gathering to celebrate Samson's downfall, so they brought blind Samson to the temple to shame him. Samson stood between two pillars that held up the temple the people were meeting in. And when Samson prayed to God for one more burst of strength, God answered in a powerful way.** Read aloud Judges 16:28, then continue: **Samson's strength returned, and with one mighty push he brought down the pillars. The entire temple area caved in and killed Samson along with the Philistines! What a final feat of strength!** Read aloud Exodus 15:2. Ask:

➤ *Why do you think God made Samson strong once more?*

➤ *Where was Samson's true strength?*

➤ *How did Samson's repentance to God play a role in his becoming strong again?*

➤ *In what ways is God our strength?*

Say: **Just as Samson learned his true strength was in God and not his hair, we know our strength is in God and not in lucky pennies. Samson's hair was the symbol of his promise to God, but his real strength was in God himself!** Read aloud Exodus 15:2 and repeat the relay once more, this time without using the "lucky items." When kids pick up the balloon barbells, have them shout, "My strength is in the Lord my God!"

Distribute the Who's Who Samson cards and invite a volunteer to read the card aloud. Punch holes in the corners of the cards and add them to the kids' Who's Who flip rings. If there's time, review any cards previously collected.

Who Was ABIGAIL?

Matthew 5:9

Simple Supplies: You'll need a Bible, paper plates, plastic spoons, modeling dough or florist's clay, scissors, rubber bands, tape, and copies of the Who's Who Abigail card from page 46.

Before class, collect a paper plate, a walnut-sized lump of modeling dough or florist's clay, two plastic spoons, and a rubber band for each person plus a set of items for yourself. Make a flying dove by placing a small clump of modeling dough in the bowl of one spoon. Place a second spoon over the first to hide the clay, then wrap a rubber band securely around the base of the bowls. Cut a paper plate in half and tape one of the halves across the handles of the spoons with the rounded side of the plate pointing toward the ends of the handles to make the dove's wings. (Be sure to tape the plate to the handles securely!) Cut the other paper plate half into thirds and tape one of the pie-shaped portions to the underside of the rounded plate to make the dove's tail. (You can toss out the other two-thirds of the plate.) Finally, use permanent markers to make eyes and a beak. (Since the bird's head is weighted, it should fly fairly well when sailed as a paper airplane.) Write the name "Abigail" on the Who's Who board (directions on page 4) or on the chalkboard.

THE WHO & THE WHY

Have kids stand opposite you and about ten feet away. Hold the flying dove and say: **This is a beautiful white bird. Can anyone tell me what kind of bird this is?** Allow kids to respond and tell you're holding a dove.

Continue: **Doves are known for the long distances they can fly. Let' see how far this dove can fly. I'll give it a launch, and if the dove flies to you, try to catch it.** Fly the dove several times, then say: **Doves are known for their flying ability, but they're also known as something else. Doves are known as symbols of peace. There were many peacemakers in the Bible, but one woman was an especially skillful peacemaker. This peacemaker's name was Abigail, and because she was a peace-loving person, she saved many lives. Let's discover who Abigail was, then we'll make flying doves to see how far your doves can fly.**

Long ago during Old Testament times, a beautiful woman named Abigail was married to a mean man named Nabal. Unfortunately, Nabal was stingy, mean spirited, and never minded a fight. King David sent one of his men to Nabal to ask for food for God's soldiers. **What do you think Nabal said?** Pause. **No! No food for you!** Even though Nabal was very rich, he refused to give King David and his men food. When King David heard this, he was very angry and told his men to put on their swords, that they would fight and kill Nabal and his household.

When Abigail heard of this, she collected a feast and told Nabal nothing. Abigail hurried to King David and shared the food with David and his men. Abigail apologized for her mean-spirited husband and asked for David's forgiveness. King David forgave Nabal, and a great disaster was stopped because Abigail had made peace. Nabal was struck dead by God a few days later, and Abigail became King David's wife. God rewarded her richly for being his peacemaker. Read aloud Matthew 5:9, then ask:

> ➤ *In what ways did Abigail make peace between King David and her mean husband, Nabal?*
> ➤ *Why is being a peacemaker important?*
> ➤ *How can we bring peace to the people and situations around us?*

Say: **Abigail prevented a terrible fight between Nabal and King David and saved her mean husband's life, even though he had caused the trouble. We can be peacemakers like Abigail, too, even when someone else has caused trouble. God wants us to bring peace to each other and to the world. Seeing how far a dove can fly is fun. But seeing how far we can go to make peace is better!**

Hand out the craft materials and show kids how to make their own flying doves. Then have dove races as you see how far the doves can fly across the room. When the races are over, distribute the Who's Who Abigail cards and invite a volunteer to read the card aloud. Punch holes in the corners of the cards and add them to the kids' Who's Who flip rings. If there's time, review any cards previously collected.

Who Was SARAH ? ? ? ?

Genesis 21:1-3; Matthew 19:26

Simple Supplies: You'll need a Bible, two paper lunch sacks, scissors, tape, and copies of the Sarah and baby Isaac patterns from page 44. You'll also need copies of the Who's Who Sarah card from page 48.

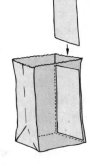

Before class, prepare the secret sack by cutting the side off one of the lunch sacks. Tuck the strip of sack inside the other lunch sack, matching up the bottom and sides. Tape the false side in place along the sides and bottom but leave the top edge open so it creates a secret pocket flap. You'll place the picture of baby Isaac in the secret flap before message time. During message time, hold the top of the sack closed to seal off the secret flap, then let the flap open at the appropriate time to let baby Isaac tumble out. Finally, write the name "Sarah" on the Who's Who board (directions on page 4) or on the chalkboard.

THE WHO & THE WHY

Place the pattern for Sarah beside you and hold the secret sack with the flap tightly closed. (Be sure the picture of baby Isaac is hidden in the flap.) Say: **Have you ever thought that something was impossible and then it happened? How did you feel?** Encourage kids to tell their experiences, then say: **You probably remember the story from long ago in Old Testament times of Abraham and how he followed God from his home in Ur. Abraham was married to a beautiful woman named Sarah.**

Hold up the figure of Sarah, then continue: **But before their names were changed to Abraham and Sarah, their names were Abram and Sarai. Abram loved Sarai very much, and the two wanted a family to love as well. Year after year they waited, but there was no baby for Sarai and Abram. Sarai had loyally followed Abram on the journey God led them on. She had even pretended to be his sister when a king wanted to marry her and Abram was afraid the king would kill him to marry Sarai.**

But though Sarai was loyal to Abram and God, she had no baby. Sarai thought it would be impossible to have a baby when she reached the age of ninety. Only young woman had babies, didn't they?

One day, three angels visited Abram and Sarai. They sat down outside the tent. Show kids the empty inside of the sack, then hold it on its side on the floor like a tent. The visitors told Abram that he and Sarai would have a baby within the year. Sarai had gone into the tent to prepare dinner (drop the picture of Sarah into the sack, but not into the flap pocket), but she could still hear what the visitors had said, and she laughed! Why do you think Sarai laughed at having a baby?

Pause for responses, then continue: Sarai thought it was impossible and even funny to think of herself having a baby at her age. But nothing is impossible with God! God changed Abram's name to Abraham, and he changed Sarai's name to Sarah. And within a year, something wonderful happened!

Flip the flap to the other side of the sack to keep the picture of Sarah from falling out, then let the picture of baby Isaac tumble out. Sarah and Abraham had a baby boy whom they named Isaac because the name Isaac means "laughter." Sarah learned that nothing is impossible with God! Read aloud Genesis 21:1-3 and Matthew 19:26. Then ask:

➤ *Why did Sarah think it was impossible for her to have a baby?*

➤ *In what ways did Sarah's faith grow when she finally held baby Isaac?*

➤ *How is trusting in God a way to demonstrate our love for him?*

Say: Sarah lived to be a very old woman of 127 years old. But as long as Sarah lived, she grew in faith and love for God, who had given her the "impossible" gift of a son!

Distribute the Who's Who Sarah cards and invite a volunteer to read the card aloud. Punch holes in the corners of the cards and add them to the kids' Who's Who flip rings. If there's time, review any Who's Who cards previously collected.

Who Was SOLOMON ???

1 Kings 3:5, 9-14; 4:29-31

Simple Supplies: You'll need a Bible, ice-cream containers (the barrel type from an ice-cream shop, one for each child plus one extra), glitter glue, plastic jewels, brown grocery sacks, markers, scissors, tape, 2-by-4-inch strips of construction paper, and copies of the Who's Who Solomon card from page 48.

Before class, collect ice-cream barrels and wash and dry the insides. Take one barrel and cover it with brown paper from a grocery sack. Color the paper to look like a brick or stone well. If you'd like, add a brown construction-paper handle. Cut the paper strips kids will use during message time. Finally, write the name "Solomon" on the Who's Who board (directions on page 4) or on the chalkboard.

THE WHO & THE WHY

Place the ice-cream-container "wishing well" in the center of the floor and gather kids around the well. Distribute slips of paper and markers or pencils. Say: **Let's pretend you could have one of these wishes come true: you could be very wise or very, very rich. Which would you wish for? Think about your reasons, then write your answer on the slip of paper and place it in this wishing well.** When all of the slips are in the wishing well, tally the votes for each wish to discover the winner. (Chances are, your class will vote on wishing for riches.) Ask:

➤ *What are reasons to wish for riches? to wish for wisdom?*

➤ *Which can help people more? Why?*

Say: **You might have had a tough time choosing your wish. In the Old Testament, we read about King David's son Solomon, who became king after his father died. God told Solomon he could have any wish, and Solomon decided that wisdom to help his people and serve God was more important than great wealth. God was so pleased with his wish that he made Solomon both wise *and* rich. In fact, King Solomon is known as the wisest and richest man who ever lived!** Read aloud 1 Kings 3:5, 9-14 and 4:29-31. Then say: **God honored Solomon's desire for wisdom and justice and still gave him riches beyond measure. Solomon wisely used the gifts God had given him. He ruled God's people with wisdom and his wealth to build an awesome temple in Jerusalem that was built to honor God.** Ask:

➤ *In what ways did Solomon use his great wisdom to help others? to serve God?*

➤ *Why do you think God was pleased that Solomon asked for wisdom to rule God's people instead of personal wealth or a long life?*

Say: **Solomon was wiser than he thought when he told God he desired great wisdom to rule in fairness and kindness. But God added** to his wisdom, and Solomon never stopped thanking and worshiping God for his precious gift! We can thank and honor God, too, by making Worship Wells to hold notes of thanks, praise, and prayer to God.

Let kids decorate the ice-cream containers using the craft items. Then invite kids to write a brief thank-you to God for the gifts he has given them. Read the thank-yous in a prayer and end with a corporate "amen." Have kids drop their thank-yous into their Worship Wells. Encourage them to add something to honor, thank, or praise God each day for the next two weeks.

Distribute the Who's Who Solomon cards and invite a volunteer to read the card aloud. Punch holes in the corners of the cards and add them to the kids' Who's Who flip rings. If there's time, review any Who's Who cards previously collected.

Who Was JOSIAH ? ? ? ?

Leviticus 18:4; 2 Kings 23:3

Simple Supplies: You'll need a Bible, newspapers, masking tape, a red marker, and copies of the Who's Who Josiah card from page 47.

Before class, tear sheets of newspaper in half, then use a red marker to write the words to Leviticus 18:4 across one of the halves. Wad up the papers loosely. (Be sure you have at least twenty paper wads.) Place a masking-tape line across the center of the floor and clear a playing area on each side of the line. Finally, write the name "Josiah" on the Who's Who board (directions on page 4) or on the chalkboard.

THE WHO & THE WHY

Form two teams and have teams stand on opposite sides of the masking-tape line. Divide the paper wads equally between the two teams. Explain that the object of this cleaning game is to have no paper wads on your side of the line when time is called. Tell kids they may toss paper wads back and forth over the line as quickly as possible (no throwing allowed—just gentle tossing) and that they will have three minutes to toss and keep their area clean. Begin the game and call time after three minutes. Count the paper wads on each side of the line, then give each other high fives for a cleaning job well done.

Say: **You worked together well to clean your area, and though you had paper wads coming and going, you kept working. This reminds me of young King Josiah, who had his men work to clean God's temple and** put it back in repair so it honored God. You see, Josiah was the son and grandson of two men who were wicked and allowed the worship of idols in the land of Judah, where they were kings. When Josiah's wicked father was killed and Josiah was only eight years old, he became king. Josiah wasn't like his wicked father or grandfather—Josiah loved God. And because King Josiah loved God, he wanted to destroy all shrines and places of idol worship in the land. After the shrines were gone, King Josiah wanted the temple in Jerusalem cleaned and repaired. While his men worked, they discovered a lost scroll containing God's Word and his Law. Did anyone find anything special when they were cleaning the papers from their areas?

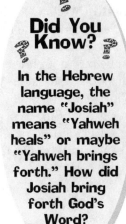

Did You Know?

In the Hebrew language, the name "Josiah" means "Yahweh heals" or maybe "Yahweh brings forth." How did Josiah bring forth God's Word?

If someone noticed the paper with Leviticus 18:4 on it, have him retrieve the paper but not read it yet. If no one saw the paper, have kids go on a "treasure hunt" to find it, but don't read the verse aloud yet.

When the paper has been found, continue: **When the words on the scroll were read to King Josiah, he was so sad that he mourned. To think the people had neglected and ignored God's Word and disobeyed God all these years! Josiah called together all the people at the temple and read the scroll to them. What did the scroll say?**

Invite a volunteer to read the paper with the Scripture verse aloud. Say: **The scroll told of the importance of obeying God and of worshiping only him. It contained what is often called the Law, including the Ten Commandments that God had long ago given to Moses. King Josiah ordered the people to obey God and to worship only him. Josiah not only cleaned God's house and honored God by doing so, he also brought back God's Word and Law to his people!** Read aloud 2 Kings 23:3, then ask:

➤ *In what ways was cleaning the temple an act of love and devotion to God?*

➤ *Why do you think Josiah felt so bad when the scroll of God's Law was read to him?*

➤ *How did King Josiah help his people by revealing the scroll to them?*

Distribute the Who's Who Josiah cards and invite a volunteer to read the card aloud. Punch holes in the corners of the cards and add them to the kids' Who's Who flip rings. If there's time, review any Who's Who cards previously collected.

Who Was NOAH ???

Genesis 6:9, 13, 14

Simple Supplies: You'll need a Bible, scissors, colored markers, a black permanent marker (fine tipped), and a 2-by-3-foot rectangle of clear vinyl (from a craft or fabric store). You'll also need copies of the Who's Who Noah card from page 47.

Before class, draw a large rainbow on the vinyl rectangle using markers in the following colors: red, orange, yellow, green, blue, and purple. Stick the vinyl to a window to draw the rainbow, then place the "virtual rainbow" in a window in the classroom. (If you would like kids to make their own Rainbow of Virtues, purchase extra clear vinyl and cut a 2-foot square for each child.) Finally, write the name "Noah" on the Who's Who board (directions on page 4) or on the chalkboard.

THE WHO & THE WHY

Gather kids in front of your virtual rainbow on the window. Hold the black fine-tipped permanent marker. Say: **I have here a virtual rainbow; that is, this rainbow almost looks like the real thing. See the bright colors? Let's use this marker to write the first letter of each color on the rainbow.** Have kids identify the colors and write a letter "R" on the left side of the red stripe, the letter "O" on the left side of the orange stripe, and so on. (Use the letter "P" for purple on the last stripe.)

After the letters are in place, say: **Long ago in Old Testament times, there were no rainbows. In fact, the first rainbow didn't appear until after God appeared to a man named Noah and told him to build a huge boat or an "ark." We'll use our virtual rainbow to discover what rainbow of virtues Noah had that pleased God and saved his life, his family's lives, and the lives of the animals in the world.**

At the time God told Noah to build the ark, Noah was the only right-eous man on earth. In other words, Noah was the only man who loved God and obeyed him with all his heart. Let's write the word "righteous" on the "R" stripe. Write the word "righteous" on the red stripe, using the "R" as the first letter. **God told Noah he would cleanse the earth with a huge flood and kill everything in it except Noah, his family, and two of every animal. Noah listened to God, then built the ark. Noah was righteous, and he was also obedient.** Write the word "obedient" after the letter O on the orange stripe. **God sent two of every animal to the ark, and Noah and his family cared for them during the forty days and nights of flooding**

rains. **Noah must have been very tired at times, but he always put God and his care for the animals first. In other words, Noah yielded to God's will.** Write the word "yielded" after the letter Y on the yellow stripe.

After about a year, the flood waters went down, and God told Noah and his family to rebuild the world and populate it. God had kept his promise to keep them all safe. The first thing Noah did was to build an altar to thank God for his grace. **Noah was grateful for God's great love and power!** Write the word "grateful" after the letter G on the green stripe. **Noah had been righteous, obedient, yielding, and grateful. And through all the days and months on the ark, Noah trusted God and was brave.** Write the word "brave" after the letter B on the blue stripe. **And what else had Noah been? Noah had been patient and waited on God for his timing and his will.** Write the word "patient" after the letter P on the purple stripe. **And because Noah had been such a rainbow of virtues, God made another promise: God promised never again to destroy the entire world by flooding it. God placed a rainbow in the sky as a sign of his powerful promise.** Invite kids to read the virtues Noah demonstrated from the words on the rainbow. Then ask:

➤ *How did all of these virtues help Noah draw close to God?*
➤ *In what ways did these virtues save Noah and his family?*
➤ *What are ways we can nurture these same virtues in our own lives?*

If there's time, let kids make their own Rainbow of Virtues to hang in their windows at home as reminders of the virtues we want to grow in our lives. Then distribute the Who's Who Noah cards and invite a volunteer to read the card aloud. Punch holes in the corners of the cards and add them to the kids' Who's Who flip rings. If there's time, review any cards previously collected.

Who Was HANNAH?

Matthew 19:26; 2 Peter 3:9

Simple Supplies: You'll need a Bible, tacky craft glue, and one each of the following for every person plus one extra set: a small red felt heart, a small bandage, a small scroll with a rubber band, and a small craft teddy bear. You'll also need copies of the Who's Who Hannah card from page 47.

Before class, collect the items listed above. To make each small scroll, simply cut a 3-by-2-inch piece of paper and roll it into a scroll, then slip a rubber band around to secure the scroll. (If you have young children, you may wish to write, "God keeps his promises" on the scrolls. Older kids will write their own scrolls.) Finally, write the name "Hannah" on the Who's Who board (directions on page 4) or on the chalkboard.

THE WHO & THE WHY

Hold up a teddy bear and say: **This teddy bear reminds me of a special bear I had when I was a child. I loved my bear very much and slept with him every night. But when I was a bit older, people told me I should give teddy up and not sleep with him any longer because I was too old for such a thing. Do you have any special toys that would be hard to give up for any reason?** Encourage kids to share their experiences, then say: **In the Old Testament, we read about a woman named Hannah who wanted a child so badly. Let's use these special bears to learn about Hannah and about how she gave up her most precious thing in life.** Distribute the teddy bears and have the other items handy.

Hannah was married to a man named Elkanah who loved her very much. But while Hannah had no child to love or hold, Elkanah's other wife, Peninnah, had many children. Peninnah made fun of Hannah and teased her until Hannah would cry and refuse to eat. One day while Hannah was at the shrine at Shiloh to give thanks to God, she asked God for a son and vowed to dedicate her son to serving God. God heard Hannah's prayer and answered by giving her a son whom she named Samuel. Oh, how Hannah loved Samuel! Let's add a heart to our bears to show how much Hannah loved Samuel.

Glue a small red heart to the front of each bear. Then continue: **When Samuel was still a young boy, Hannah remembered her prayer to dedicate Samuel to God's service. And though it was hard to give Samuel up, Hannah took Samuel to Eli the priest so Samuel could learn about God and how to serve him. Let's add a scroll of God's Word to the bears to show how Hannah wanted Samuel to learn about serving God.**

Have older kids write "God keeps his promises" on the scrolls, then attach the scrolls to the bears' front legs using the rubber bands. Continue: **Think of how hard it must have been to give Samuel up! Hannah must have felt great pain because she loved Samuel and wanted him close to her. But God made Hannah glad for her son, and she willingly gave Samuel up so he could serve God—which he did for his entire life! Let's add a bandage**

to symbolize how giving up to God is sometimes hard but is always worth it! Add a bandage to the bears, then ask:

> ➤ *In what ways did God show his love for Hannah?*
> ➤ *Why do you think Hannah kept her promise to God?*
> ➤ *Think of how much Hannah loved Samuel, and how she gave Samuel up so he could serve God. What does this tell us about how much Hannah loved God?*
> ➤ *How can we be willing to sacrifice for God and keep our promises to him?*

Read aloud Matthew 19:26 and 2 Peter 3:9. Say: **Hannah discovered that with God nothing is impossible and that he always keeps his promises. Hannah also learned that we must be willing to keep our promises to God as well. For when we keep our promises to God, we are telling him that we love him!** Have kids hold their teddy bears and share a prayer thanking God for helping us keep our promises to him just as Hannah did. End with a corporate "amen." Tell kids to hold their bears each night for a week as they offer up their own prayers of thanksgiving to God for his gifts to us. Then distribute the Who's Who Hannah cards and invite a volunteer to read the card aloud. Punch holes in the corners of the cards and add them to the kids' Who's Who flip rings. If there's time, review any cards previously collected.

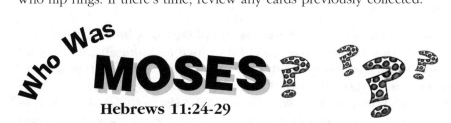

Who Was MOSES?
Hebrews 11:24-29

Simple Supplies: You'll need a Bible, disposable aluminum pie plates, fishing line, scissors, a nail for each child plus one for yourself, and the following items: a hammer, a pair of pliers, a cotton swab, and a crayon. You'll also need copies of the Who's Who Moses card from page 47.
Before class, collect the items. Be sure you have a pie plate for each child plus one for yourself. Finally, write the name "Moses" on the Who's Who board (directions on page 4) or on the chalkboard.

THE WHO & THE WHY

Set out the hammer, pliers, cotton swab, one nail, and a crayon. Hold one of the pie plates and say: **I want to make a nifty design on this pie plate. I want to poke holes through it, so I need to find just the right tool for the job. Look over these tools. Which one do you think is the best choice for the job and why?**

Allow kids to share their ideas (the nail is the answer, of course), then briefly discuss why the hammer, pliers, cotton swab, and crayon are not the best choices for the job of poking holes through the pie plate. Say: **It's important to use the correct tool to get the job done. God knows this when he calls us for special plans he has. In the Old Testament, God called Moses for many special jobs because God saw in Moses his perfect tool to accomplish his plans. Let's discover more about Moses, then we'll use these nails and pie plates to complete our own projects. As you learn about Moses, keep track of the jobs he was called to do by God.** Hand each person a pie plate and a nail to set on the floor.

Moses was born a Hebrew slave in the country of Egypt, but when his mother learned that all baby Hebrew boys were to be killed by Pharaoh, she put him in a basket on a river and trusted God to save Moses. Pharaoh's daughter pulled baby Moses from the water and raised him as an Egyptian. But when Moses was an adult, he returned to his own people, the Hebrews. Then God called to Moses on a hillside in a bush that didn't burn up and told him to go to Pharaoh to free the Hebrew slaves.

This was the first important job Moses did, and he obeyed God all the way. The next job Moses was called to do was to lead the freed Israelites across the Red Sea. Again, Moses obeyed and followed God's leading. Moses' next job was to pray for the Israelites and to take their needs to God. Moses prayed for food and water for his people, and God answered. Moses' fourth important job was to climb Mount Sinai to receive the Ten Commandments, which God gave for his people to follow. Again Moses obeyed and completed the job God called him to do. Moses spent his entire life living as God's special tool in completing God's will. Read aloud Hebrews 11:24-29, then ask:

> ➤ *In what ways did Moses' obedience to God help him be a good and effective tool?*
> ➤ *How does our own obedience to God help us serve him?*
> ➤ *What jobs does God call us as Christians to do?*

Say: **Moses' life was long, and he was dedicated to being God's tool. Because of the love in Moses' heart, his obedience, and the way he listened to God's orders, Moses gave us a wonderful example of becoming powerful tools in God's hands! Now let's use our correct tools to complete a fun project to remind us about being willing to be used by God in his plans.**

Explain that kids will use their nails to punch out the letters to spell "God's Tool" on their pie plates. Show kids where to begin punching the letter G and remind kids that the holes need to be close together. Finish by punching holes at the top of each pie plate and tying a 12-inch length of fishing line through the holes to make hanging loops. Tell kids to hang their projects in a sunny window to let the light shine through as a reminder of the importance of being God's tools each day.

Distribute the Who's Who Moses cards and invite a volunteer to read the card aloud. Punch holes in the corners of the cards and add them to the kids' Who's Who flip rings. If there's time, review any Who's Who cards previously collected.

Who Were The 12 TRIBES?

Genesis 49:2-28

Simple Supplies: You'll need a Bible, scissors, markers, paper clips, a hole punch, tape, colored construction paper (white, blue, red, green, and orange), modeling dough, a large plastic cup, and a medium-sized tree branch (with several twigs sticking out from it). You'll also need copies of the Who's Who Twelve Tribes card from page 48.

Before class, cut 2-by-3-inch cards from construction paper. Cut the cards as follows: one white card, six blue cards, two orange cards, two red cards, and two green cards. Use a paper punch to make a hole in the top center of every card except the white one. On the white card, write the name "Jacob" and below the name write "Israel." Place a large clump of modeling dough in the bottom of the plastic cup and stick the end of the branch in the dough to hold it upright. Be sure you have twelve paper clips. Finally, write "12 Tribes" on the Who's Who board (directions on page 4) or on the chalkboard.

THE WHO & THE WHY

Place the "tree" in the center of the room. Say: **It's nice to be one whole class of people joining together, but sometimes it's also good to be divided into groups where each group has a special job to do. God's people were one group at about the time of Abraham, and they were called Hebrews. The Hebrews were known to other people as ones who worshiped only God. Now Abraham's grandson was named Jacob, and Jacob loved God very much. Jacob had children with several wives, which was fine back in Old Testament times. The names of the mothers of Jacob's** children were Leah, Rachel, Bilhah, and Zilpah. God had promised Jacob that his sons and their children would become a great nation called Israel. God changed Jacob's name to Israel, and so began the family tree of the Israelites.

Tape the white card with Jacob's name to the trunk of the tree branch. Say: **The Israelites were Hebrews, and they were God's people, but from the time of Jacob onward they were known as Israelites. Jacob had twelve sons and their families, so they were split into family groups, or tribes, and became the twelve tribes of Israel. In other words, they were the twelve family groups descended from Jacob. Each group was given a different job to do. Some of them were fighters, others were farmers, some were priests, and others were kingly rulers. Let's split into groups of our own as we learn more about the twelve tribes of Israel.**

Form four groups and hand one group the blue cards, one group the orange cards, one the red cards, and one group the green cards. Assign each group the following verses to read and have them list the sons of each woman on their cards, one name per card.

> ➤ *Leah's sons: Genesis 35:23* (blue cards)
> ➤ *Rachel's sons: Genesis 35:24* (green cards)
> ➤ *Bilhah's sons: Genesis 35:25* (orange cards)
> ➤ *Zilpah's sons: Genesis 35:36* (red cards)

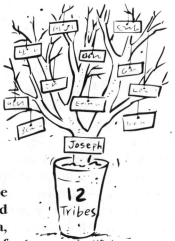

After the cards are complete, have children place paper clips through the holes and hang them from the branches of the family tree. Clump the colors together on branches as closely as possible. Then read the names of the twelve tribes of Israel (and Genesis 49:2-28, if there's time). Say: **God had a plan for this great nation and gave special roles to several of the tribes. From the tribe of Judah would come mighty King David and then later on, through Mary, Jesus. From the tribe of the Levites came priests such as Eli and Samuel. Each tribe lived in a different area, and together they grew into the nation of Israel. But it didn't stop there! When Jesus** came to save and love us, he brought all of God's people together into a group we know as Christians. And just as the Hebrews and Israelites were God's people, so are we! Ask:

> ➤ *How is having different groups coming together as one similar to different people in our church coming together as one?*

➤ *What responsibilities do we have living as God's people?*

Say: **God's nation of people began with Abraham and the Hebrews. It continued with Jacob becoming Israel and establishing the twelve tribes to become the nation of Israel. And it continues today with Christians all over the world being God's people.**

Distribute the Who's Who Twelve Tribes cards and invite a volunteer to read the card aloud. Punch holes in the corners of the cards and add them to the kids' Who's Who flip rings. If there's time, review any Who's Who cards previously collected.

Who Was ESTHER?

John 15:13

Simple Supplies: You'll need a Bible, pictures of extinct animals, and copies of the Who's Who Esther card from page 46

Before class, collect one or more pictures of extinct animals such as a wooly mammoth and dinosaurs. Finally, write the name "Queen Esther" on the Who's Who board (directions on page 4) or on the chalkboard.

THE WHO & THE WHY

Hold up the pictures of the extinct animals and ask kids to tell what the pictures have in common. After kids tell their ideas, say: **These are pictures of animals that are extinct. That means that these animals aren't alive any longer and will never live again. It's sad to think that once these animals were alive and roaming the world but are now gone. In the Old Testament, a brave and smart woman stopped a horrible tragedy from making her *people* extinct.**

Esther was a beautiful woman who was also a Jew or Hebrew—one of God's people. Esther was so beautiful that she caught the eye of a king in a foreign land who married her and made her Queen Esther. The king didn't realize that his beloved queen was a Jew. Now in the kingdom there was a nasty man named Haman who wanted all of the Jews put to death. He wanted all of God's people killed because they would not bow down to worship false gods and they showed no fear. Haman tricked the king into agreeing to kill the Jews. When Queen Esther discovered what was going to happen, she slyly went to the king and requested that he and Haman come to a special banquet she would prepare. While they were at the banquet, the king asked Queen Esther what she would like.

The king promised Queen Esther that anything she wanted he would do for her. So what do you think Queen Esther asked for?

Allow kids to tell their ideas, then continue: **Queen Esther told the king a cruel man wanted all of her people killed. When the king asked who this evil man was, Queen Esther pointed to Haman. In the end, the king saved the Jews and had Haman hanged instead for his evil plans. Queen Esther had saved God's people from extinction through her bravery, faith, and wise actions!** Ask:

➤ *In what ways was Queen Esther brave? wise? faithful?*
➤ *Why do you think Queen Esther placed herself in danger by admitting to the king that she was a Jew?*

Read aloud John 15:13, then ask:

➤ *Why is the willingness to die for one's people a demonstration of love?*
➤ *How was this a sign of Queen Esther's love for her people? for God?*

Did You Know?

Esther's name in Persian means "star." Queen Esther certainly was a superstar when it came to loving and saving her people!

Say: **Queen Esther was very brave to put herself and her life on the line for people she may not have even known. But just think of how awful it would have been for a nation of God's people to have all been killed and become extinct! What a sad world it would have been. Yet because of Queen Esther's great love for her own people and for God's people in general, she risked it all and was greatly rewarded!**

Distribute the Who's Who Esther cards and invite a volunteer to read the card aloud. Punch holes in the corners of the cards and add them to kids' Who's Who flip rings. If there's time, review any Who's Who cards previously collected.

SAMUEL

Trust in the LORD with all your heart and lean not on your own understanding; in all your ways acknowledge him, and he will make your paths straight. (Proverbs 3:5, 6)

Trust in the LORD with all your heart and lean not on your own understanding; in all your ways acknowledge him, and he will make your paths straight. (Proverbs 3:5, 6)

SARAH

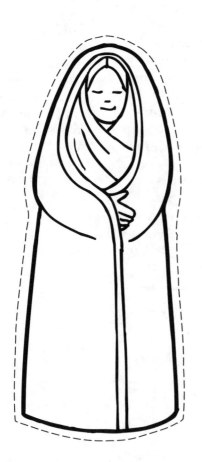
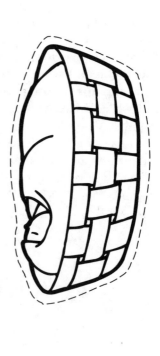

BALAAM

WHO'S WHO CARDS

Abigail

Abigail brought peace between mighty King David and her sour husband, Nabal. Abigail taught us the value of being God's peacemakers. (1 Samuel 25)

Abraham

Abram's name was changed to Abraham when God promised he would become a great nation and his descendants would be as numerous as the stars in the heavens. (Genesis 17:5, 6)

Balaam

Balaam was a stubborn man who questioned God and wouldn't accept God's answers. Balaam's donkey talked to him, then an angel warned Balaam to speak only God's words. (Numbers 22)

Daniel

Daniel refused to worship or pray to false gods and so was sent to the lions' den. Daniel prayed, and God answered by sending an angel to close the mouths of the lions. (Daniel 6)

David

David, the youngest of seven sons, defeated the giant Goliath when he was a young lad. Samuel anointed David as the next king of Israel because God saw David as a man after his own heart. (1 Samuel 16)

Deborah

Deborah was a woman judge whom God called to help win an important battle. Deborah was brave and went to battle when her general was afraid to go alone. (Judges 4)

Esther

Esther was a beautiful woman who became queen in a country that didn't worship God. Evil Haman decided to kill the Jews, but Esther exposed his plans and saved God's people from being killed. (Esther 7)

Gideon

Gideon was a simple farmer called by God to lead a battle. Gideon asked God for a sign, then collected his 300 soldiers and defeated God's enemy by making a terrible noise in the night. (Judges 6)

WHO'S WHO CARDS

Hannah OT

Childless Hannah was teased by Peninnah. Hannah promised to dedicate her son to God if he would give her a child. When God gave Hannah a son, she sent Samuel to serve the Lord. (1 Samuel 1; 2)

Job OT

Job was a righteous man but was tested by Satan's evil. Job refused to curse God even when his family, flocks, and wealth were taken away. God rewarded Job's faith and doubled his wealth. (Job 42:10-17)

Joseph OT

Joseph was his father's favorite son. Jealous, Joseph's brothers sold him into slavery but years later came to ask for food. Joseph forgave his brothers and taught us the healing power of forgiveness. (Genesis 50)

Josiah OT

Josiah, who became king at age 8, spent his life cleaning God's temple and destroying false idols. Josiah discovered God's long-lost laws and brought them back to his people so God could be obeyed. (2 Kings 22)

Methuselah OT

Methuselah was the oldest living person on earth and in recorded history. He lived to the ripe old age of 969, far more than Adam, Noah, Abraham, or Moses. (Genesis 5:25-27)

Moses OT

Moses was born a Hebrew but was raised in Egypt. God called upon Moses to lead God's people out of bondage in Egypt. Moses delivered God's Ten Commandments to the Israelites. (Exodus 2)

Naomi OT

Naomi befriended her daughter-in-law Ruth and taught her about God. Naomi and Ruth helped each other all their lives, giving us a perfect example of friendship and shared love for God. (Ruth 1:16-18)

Noah OT

Noah was the only righteous man in the world when God told him to build an ark because of the flood God would send. Because of Noah's trust and obedience, his family and the animals were saved. (Genesis 6)

WHO'S WHO CARDS

Prophets
OT

Prophets were often common people chosen by God to reveal his messages and will to others. Prophets sometimes relayed God's messages in unusual ways. (Numbers 12:6)

Rahab
OT

Rahab lived in Jericho and helped hide God's soldier spies. In return for her incredible faith, God saved Rahab's life and those of her family. (Joshua 2)

Samson
OT

Samson was a Hebrew judge whose strength left him after he broke his vows to God. But God returned his strength one last time after Samson repented and asked for help to defeat the Philistines. (Judges 16)

Samuel
OT

Young Samuel was dedicated to God and learned early to listen and obey God. Samuel was both a priest and a prophet and was the one to anoint both Saul and David kings. (1 Samuel 3)

Sarah
OT

Sarah, Abraham's wife, longed for a child. When God said that Sarah would have a baby at age 90, Sarah laughed, but the laugh was on her, for God honored his promise with a boy named Isaac. (Genesis 21)

Solomon
OT

Solomon was King David's son and followed his father as king of Israel. God gave Solomon the gift of wisdom, and Solomon because the wisest and richest man in all of history. (1 Kings 3)

Twelve Tribes
OT

God changed Jacob's name to Israel and promised his descendants would become a great nation. His sons became the twelve tribes of Israel. Each tribe had a special place to live and role to play. (Genesis 35; 49)